ALABASTER

Printed in Canada

Contact
hello@alabasterco.com
www.alabasterco.com

Alabaster Co. The Bible Beautiful.
Visual imagery & thoughtful design integrated within the Bible.
Cultivating conversation between art, beauty, & faith.

Founded in 2016.

NLT.

ARTIST INTRODUCTION

———

The Book of Job highlights the story of a righteous man who is abruptly met with deep, bewildering suffering. As a unique exploration of wisdom, Job ultimately deals with ideas of theodicy—why would a good God let evil happen? Why do bad things happen to good people?

While the characters in the book try to pin Job's suffering on logical reasoning, in the end, the book does not necessarily give a straight answer. While we cannot always understand why we suffer, Job reminds us that we can choose to lament and bring our pain and grief to God, trusting in God's greatness and vast wisdom.

We explore these themes through a woeful purple, connecting ideas of pain and suffering to a color that is often reserved for royalty and righteousness. Images of decay and erosion highlight natural forces of suffering and loss. And the lighting technique known as *Chiaroscuro* is utilized to explore the ongoing tension and wrestling that Job has with God.

There is wisdom in this—that the vast cosmic God who created everything has a vantage point grander than any human understanding of justice and suffering. In the end, The Book of Job is an invitation to trust. In the midst of the perplexing, unfathomable suffering and trauma we bear as human beings may, we all choose to trust in the mystery of God. Amen.

BOOK OF

JOB

1

PROLOGUE

[1] There once was a man named Job who lived in the land of Uz. He was blameless—a man of complete integrity. He feared God and stayed away from evil. [2] He had seven sons and three daughters. [3] He owned 7,000 sheep, 3,000 camels, 500 teams of oxen, and 500 female donkeys. He also had many servants. He was, in fact, the richest person in that entire area. [4] Job's sons would take turns preparing feasts in their homes, and they would also invite their three sisters to celebrate with them. [5] When these celebrations ended—sometimes after several days—Job would purify his children. He would get up early in the morning and offer a burnt offering for each of them. For Job said to himself, "Perhaps my children have sinned and have cursed God in their hearts." This was Job's regular practice.

JOB'S FIRST TEST

⁶ One day the members of the heavenly court came to present themselves before the Lord, and the Accuser, Satan, came with them. ⁷ "Where have you come from?" the Lord asked Satan. Satan answered the Lord, "I have been patrolling the earth, watching everything that's going on." ⁸ Then the Lord asked Satan, "Have you noticed my servant Job? He is the finest man in all the earth. He is blameless—a man of complete integrity. He fears God and stays away from evil." ⁹ Satan replied to the Lord, "Yes, but Job has good reason to fear God. ¹⁰ You have always put a wall of protection around him and his home and his property. You have made him prosper in everything he does. Look how rich he is! ¹¹ But reach out and take away everything he has, and he will surely curse you to your face!" ¹² "All right, you may test him," the Lord said to Satan. "Do whatever you want with everything he possesses, but don't harm him physically." So Satan left the Lord's presence. ¹³ One day when Job's sons and daughters were feasting at the oldest brother's house, ¹⁴ a messenger arrived at Job's home with this news: "Your oxen were plowing, with the donkeys feeding beside them, ¹⁵ when the Sabeans raided us. They stole all the animals and killed all the farmhands. I am the only

one who escaped to tell you." [16] While he was still speaking, another messenger arrived with this news: "The fire of God has fallen from heaven and burned up your sheep and all the shepherds. I am the only one who escaped to tell you." [17] While he was still speaking, a third messenger arrived with this news: "Three bands of Chaldean raiders have stolen your camels and killed your servants. I am the only one who escaped to tell you." [18] While he was still speaking, another messenger arrived with this news: "Your sons and daughters were feasting in their oldest brother's home. [19] Suddenly, a powerful wind swept in from the wilderness and hit the house on all sides. The house collapsed, and all your children are dead. I am the only one who escaped to tell you." [20] Job stood up and tore his robe in grief. Then he shaved his head and fell to the ground to worship. [21] He said,

"I came naked from my mother's womb,
and I will be naked when I leave.
The Lord gave me what I had,
and the Lord has taken it away.
Praise the name of the Lord!"

[22] In all of this, Job did not sin by blaming God.

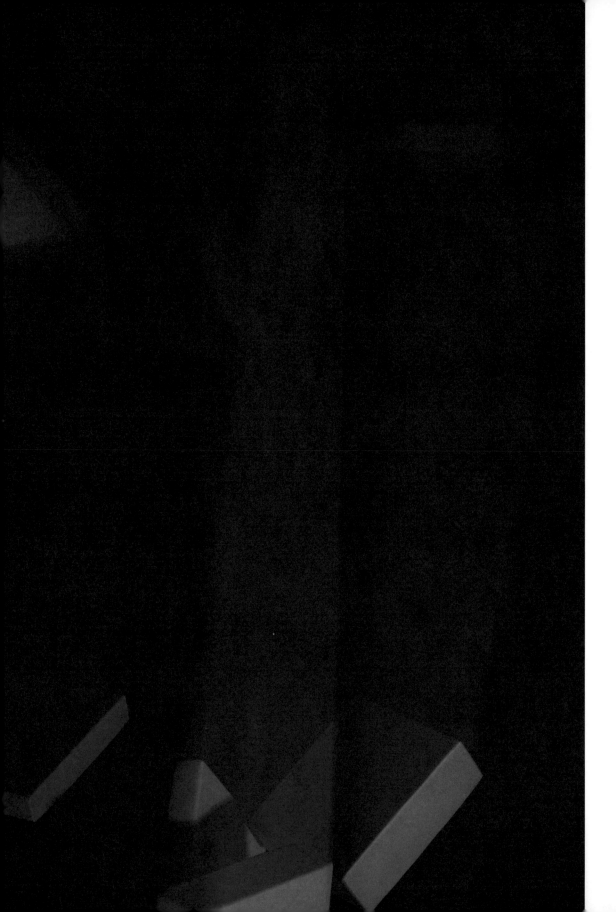

2

JOB'S SECOND TEST

¹ One day the members of the heavenly court came again to present themselves before the Lord, and the Accuser, Satan, came with them. ² "Where have you come from?" the Lord asked Satan. Satan answered the Lord, "I have been patrolling the earth, watching everything that's going on." ³ Then the Lord asked Satan, "Have you noticed my servant Job? He is the finest man in all the earth. He is blameless—a man of complete integrity. He fears God and stays away from evil. And he has maintained his integrity, even though you urged me to harm him without cause." ⁴ Satan replied to the Lord, "Skin for skin! A man will give up everything he has to save his life. ⁵ But reach out and take away his health, and he will surely curse you to your face!" ⁶ "All right, do with him as you please," the Lord said to Satan. "But spare his life." ⁷ So Satan left the Lord's presence, and he struck Job with terrible boils from head to foot. ⁸ Job scraped his skin with a piece of broken pottery as he sat among the ashes. ⁹ His wife said to him, "Are you still trying to maintain your integrity? Curse God and die." ¹⁰ But Job replied, "You talk like a foolish woman. Should we accept only good things from the hand of God and never anything bad?" So in all this, Job said nothing wrong.

JOB'S THREE FRIENDS SHARE HIS ANGUISH

¹¹ When three of Job's friends heard of the tragedy he had suffered, they got together and traveled from their homes to comfort and console him. Their names were Eliphaz the Temanite, Bildad the Shuhite, and Zophar the Naamathite. ¹² When they saw Job from a distance, they scarcely recognized him. Wailing loudly, they tore their robes and threw dust into the air over their heads to show their grief. ¹³ Then they sat on the ground with him for seven days and nights. No one said a word to Job, for they saw that his suffering was too great for words.

3

JOB'S FIRST SPEECH

¹ At last Job spoke, and he cursed the day of his birth. ² He said:

³ "Let the day of my birth be erased,
and the night I was conceived.

⁴ Let that day be turned to darkness.
Let it be lost even to God on high,
and let no light shine on it.

⁵ Let the darkness and utter gloom claim that day
for its own.
Let a black cloud overshadow it,
and let the darkness terrify it.

⁶ Let that night be blotted off the calendar,
never again to be counted among the days of the year,
never again to appear among the months.

⁷ Let that night be childless.
Let it have no joy.

⁸ Let those who are experts at cursing—
whose cursing could rouse Leviathan—
curse that day.

⁹ Let its morning stars remain dark.
Let it hope for light, but in vain;
may it never see the morning light.

¹⁰ Curse that day for failing to shut my mother's womb,
for letting me be born to see all this trouble.

¹¹ Why wasn't I born dead?
Why didn't I die as I came from the womb?

¹² Why was I laid on my mother's lap?
Why did she nurse me at her breasts?

¹³ Had I died at birth, I would now be at peace.
I would be asleep and at rest.

¹⁴ I would rest with the world's kings and
prime ministers,
whose great buildings now lie in ruins.

¹⁵ I would rest with princes, rich in gold,
whose palaces were filled with silver.

¹⁶ Why wasn't I buried like a stillborn child,
like a baby who never lives to see the light?

¹⁷ For in death the wicked cause no trouble,
and the weary are at rest.

¹⁸ Even captives are at ease in death,
with no guards to curse them.

¹⁹ Rich and poor are both there,
and the slave is free from his master.

²⁰ Oh, why give light to those in misery,
and life to those who are bitter?

²¹ They long for death, and it won't come.
They search for death more eagerly than
for hidden treasure.

²² They're filled with joy when they finally die,
and rejoice when they find the grave.

²³ Why is life given to those with no future,
those God has surrounded with difficulties?

²⁴ I cannot eat for sighing;
my groans pour out like water.

²⁵ What I always feared has happened to me.
What I dreaded has come true.

²⁶ I have no peace, no quietness.
I have no rest; only trouble comes."

CHAPTER 3

4

ELIPHAZ'S FIRST RESPONSE TO JOB

¹ Then Eliphaz the Temanite replied to Job:

² "Will you be patient and let me say a word?
For who could keep from speaking out?
³ In the past you have encouraged many people;
you have strengthened those who were weak.
⁴ Your words have supported those who were falling;
you encouraged those with shaky knees.
⁵ But now when trouble strikes, you lose heart.
You are terrified when it touches you.
⁶ Doesn't your reverence for God give you confidence?
Doesn't your life of integrity give you hope?
⁷ Stop and think! Do the innocent die?
When have the upright been destroyed?
⁸ My experience shows that those who plant trouble
and cultivate evil will harvest the same.
⁹ A breath from God destroys them.
They vanish in a blast of his anger.
¹⁰ The lion roars and the wildcat snarls,
but the teeth of strong lions will be broken.
¹¹ The fierce lion will starve for lack of prey,
and the cubs of the lioness will be scattered.
¹² This truth was given to me in secret,
as though whispered in my ear.
¹³ It came to me in a disturbing vision at night,
when people are in a deep sleep.
¹⁴ Fear gripped me,
and my bones trembled.
¹⁵ A spirit swept past my face,
and my hair stood on end.
¹⁶ The spirit stopped, but I couldn't see its shape.
There was a form before my eyes.
In the silence I heard a voice say,
¹⁷ 'Can a mortal be innocent before God?
Can anyone be pure before the Creator?'
¹⁸ If God does not trust his own angels
and has charged his messengers with foolishness,
¹⁹ how much less will he trust people made of clay!
They are made of dust, crushed as easily as a moth.
²⁰ They are alive in the morning but dead by evening,
gone forever without a trace.
²¹ Their tent-cords are pulled and the tent collapses,
and they die in ignorance."

5

1 "Cry for help, but will anyone answer you?
Which of the angels will help you?

2 Surely resentment destroys the fool,
and jealousy kills the simple.

3 I have seen that fools may be successful for the
moment, but then comes sudden disaster.

4 Their children are abandoned far from help;
they are crushed in court with no one to defend them.

5 The hungry devour their harvest,
even when it is guarded by brambles.
The thirsty pant after their wealth.

6 But evil does not spring from the soil,
and trouble does not sprout from the earth.

7 People are born for trouble
as readily as sparks fly up from a fire.

8 If I were you, I would go to God
and present my case to him.

9 He does great things too marvelous to understand.
He performs countless miracles.

10 He gives rain for the earth
and water for the fields.

11 He gives prosperity to the poor
and protects those who suffer.

12 He frustrates the plans of schemers
so the work of their hands will not succeed.

13 He traps the wise in their own cleverness
so their cunning schemes are thwarted.

14 They find it is dark in the daytime,
and they grope at noon as if it were night.

¹⁵ He rescues the poor from the cutting words of the
strong, and rescues them
from the clutches of the powerful.
¹⁶ And so at last the poor have hope,
and the snapping jaws of the wicked are shut.
¹⁷ But consider the joy of those corrected by God!
Do not despise the discipline of the
Almighty when you sin.
¹⁸ For though he wounds, he also bandages.
He strikes, but his hands also heal.
¹⁹ From six disasters he will rescue you;
even in the seventh, he will keep you from evil.
²⁰ He will save you from death in time of famine,
from the power of the sword in time of war.
²¹ You will be safe from slander

and have no fear when destruction comes.
²² You will laugh at destruction and famine;
wild animals will not terrify you.
²³ You will be at peace with the stones of the field,
and its wild animals will be at peace with you.
²⁴ You will know that your home is safe.
When you survey your possessions,
nothing will be missing.
²⁵ You will have many children;
your descendants will be as plentiful as grass!
²⁶ You will go to the grave at a ripe old age,
like a sheaf of grain harvested at the proper time!
²⁷ We have studied life and found all this to be true.
Listen to my counsel,
and apply it to yourself."

6

JOB'S SECOND SPEECH: A RESPONSE TO ELIPHAZ

¹ Then Job spoke again:

² "If my misery could be weighed
and my troubles be put on the scales,
³ they would outweigh all the sands of the sea.
That is why I spoke impulsively.
⁴ For the Almighty has struck me down with his arrows.
Their poison infects my spirit.
God's terrors are lined up against me.
⁵ Don't I have a right to complain?
Don't wild donkeys bray when they find no grass,
and oxen bellow when they have no food?
⁶ Don't people complain about unsalted food?
Does anyone want the tasteless white of an egg?
⁷ My appetite disappears when I look at it;
I gag at the thought of eating it!
⁸ Oh, that I might have my request,
that God would grant my desire.
⁹ I wish he would crush me.
I wish he would reach out his hand and kill me.
¹⁰ At least I can take comfort in this:

Despite the pain,
I have not denied the words of the Holy One.
11 But I don't have the strength to endure.
I have nothing to live for.
12 Do I have the strength of a stone?
Is my body made of bronze?
13 No, I am utterly helpless,
without any chance of success.
14 One should be kind to a fainting friend,
but you accuse me without any fear of the Almighty.
15 My brothers, you have proved as unreliable
as a seasonal brook
that overflows its banks in the spring
16 when it is swollen with ice and melting snow.
17 But when the hot weather arrives, the water
disappears. The brook vanishes in the heat.
18 The caravans turn aside to be refreshed,
but there is nothing to drink, so they die.
19 The caravans from Tema search for this water;
the travelers from Sheba hope to find it.
20 They count on it but are disappointed.
When they arrive, their hopes are dashed.

CHAPTER 6

21 You, too, have given no help.
   You have seen my calamity,
   and you are afraid.
22 But why? Have I ever asked you for a gift?
   Have I begged for anything of yours for myself?
23 Have I asked you to rescue me from my enemies,
   or to save me from ruthless people?
24 Teach me, and I will keep quiet.
   Show me what I have done wrong.
25 Honest words can be painful,
   but what do your criticisms amount to?

26 Do you think your words are convincing
   when you disregard my cry of desperation?
27 You would even send an orphan
   into slavery or sell a friend.
28 Look at me!
   Would I lie to your face?
29 Stop assuming my guilt,
   for I have done no wrong.
30 Do you think I am lying?
   Don't I know the difference between
   right and wrong?

7

1 "Is not all human life a struggle?
Our lives are like that of a hired hand,

2 like a worker who longs for the shade,
like a servant waiting to be paid.

3 I, too, have been assigned months of futility,
long and weary nights of misery.

4 Lying in bed, I think, 'When will it be morning?'
But the night drags on, and I toss till dawn.

5 My body is covered with maggots and scabs.
My skin breaks open, oozing with pus.

JOB CRIES OUT TO GOD

6 "My days fly faster than a weaver's shuttle.
They end without hope.

7 O God, remember that my life is but a breath,
and I will never again feel happiness.

8 You see me now, but not for long.
You will look for me, but I will be gone.

9 Just as a cloud dissipates and vanishes,
those who die will not come back.

10 They are gone forever from their home—
never to be seen again.

11 I cannot keep from speaking.
I must express my anguish.
My bitter soul must complain.

12 Am I a sea monster or a dragon
that you must place me under guard?

13 I think, 'My bed will comfort me,
and sleep will ease my misery,'

14 but then you shatter me with dreams
and terrify me with visions.

15 I would rather be strangled—
rather die than suffer like this.

16 I hate my life and don't want to go on living.
Oh, leave me alone for my few remaining days.

17 What are people, that you should make so much of
us, that you should think of us so often?

18 For you examine us every morning
and test us every moment.

19 Why won't you leave me alone,
at least long enough for me to swallow!

20 If I have sinned, what have I done to you,
O watcher of all humanity?
Why make me your target?
Am I a burden to you?

21 Why not just forgive my sin
and take away my guilt?
For soon I will lie down in the dust and die.
When you look for me, I will be gone."

8

BILDAD'S FIRST RESPONSE TO JOB

¹ Then Bildad the Shuhite replied to Job:

² "How long will you go on like this?
You sound like a blustering wind.

³ Does God twist justice?
Does the Almighty twist what is right?

⁴ Your children must have sinned against him,
so their punishment was well deserved.

⁵ But if you pray to God
and seek the favor of the Almighty,

⁶ and if you are pure and live with integrity,
he will surely rise up and restore your happy home.

⁷ And though you started with little,
you will end with much.

⁸ Just ask the previous generation.
Pay attention to the experience of our ancestors.

⁹ For we were born but yesterday and know nothing.
Our days on earth are as fleeting as a shadow.

¹⁰ But those who came before us will teach you.
They will teach you the wisdom of old.

¹¹ Can papyrus reeds grow tall without a marsh?
Can marsh grass flourish without water?

¹² While they are still flowering, not ready to be cut,
they begin to wither more quickly than grass.

¹³ The same happens to all who forget God.
The hopes of the godless evaporate.

¹⁴ Their confidence hangs by a thread.
They are leaning on a spider's web.

¹⁵ They cling to their home for security, but it won't last.
They try to hold it tight, but it will not endure.

¹⁶ The godless seem like a lush plant growing in the
sunshine, its branches spreading across the garden.

¹⁷ Its roots grow down through a pile of stones;
it takes hold on a bed of rocks.

¹⁸ But when it is uprooted,
it's as though it never existed!

¹⁹ That's the end of its life,
and others spring up from the earth to replace it.

²⁰ But look, God will not reject a person of integrity,
nor will he lend a hand to the wicked.

²¹ He will once again fill your mouth with laughter
and your lips with shouts of joy.

²² Those who hate you will be clothed with shame,
and the home of the wicked
will be destroyed."

CHAPTER 8

9

JOB'S THIRD SPEECH: A RESPONSE TO BILDAD

[1] Then Job spoke again:

[2] "Yes, I know all this is true in principle.
But how can a person be declared innocent in God's sight?
[3] If someone wanted to take God to court,
would it be possible to answer him even once in a thousand times?
[4] For God is so wise and so mighty.
Who has ever challenged him successfully?
[5] Without warning, he moves the mountains,
overturning them in his anger.
[6] He shakes the earth from its place,
and its foundations tremble.
[7] If he commands it, the sun won't rise
and the stars won't shine.
[8] He alone has spread out the heavens
and marches on the waves of the sea.
[9] He made all the stars—the Bear and Orion, the Pleiades
and the constellations of the southern sky.
[10] He does great things too marvelous to understand.
He performs countless miracles.
[11] Yet when he comes near, I cannot see him.
When he moves by, I do not see him go.

¹² If he snatches someone in death, who can stop him?
Who dares to ask, 'What are you doing?'

¹³ And God does not restrain his anger.
Even the monsters of the sea are crushed
beneath his feet.

¹⁴ So who am I, that I should try to answer
God or even reason with him?

¹⁵ Even if I were right, I would have no
defense. I could only plead for mercy.

¹⁶ And even if I summoned him and he responded,
I'm not sure he would listen to me.

¹⁷ For he attacks me with a storm
and repeatedly wounds me without cause.

¹⁸ He will not let me catch my breath,
but fills me instead with bitter sorrows.

¹⁹ If it's a question of strength, he's the strong one.
If it's a matter of justice, who dares to
summon him to court?

²⁰ Though I am innocent, my own mouth
would pronounce me guilty.
Though I am blameless, it would prove me wicked.

²¹ I am innocent,
but it makes no difference to me—
I despise my life.

²² Innocent or wicked, it is all the same to God.
That's why I say, 'He destroys both the
blameless and the wicked.'

²³ When a plague sweeps through,
he laughs at the death of the innocent.

²⁴ The whole earth is in the hands of the wicked,
and God blinds the eyes of the judges.
If he's not the one who does it, who is?

²⁵ My life passes more swiftly than a runner.
It flees away without a glimpse of happiness.

²⁶ It disappears like a swift papyrus boat,
like an eagle swooping down on its prey.

²⁷ If I decided to forget my complaints,
to put away my sad face and be cheerful,

²⁸ I would still dread all the pain,
for I know you will not find me innocent, O God.

²⁹ Whatever happens, I will be found guilty.
So what's the use of trying?

³⁰ Even if I were to wash myself with soap
and clean my hands with lye,

³¹ you would plunge me into a muddy ditch,
and my own filthy clothing would hate me.

³² God is not a mortal like me,
so I cannot argue with him or take him to trial.

³³ If only there were a mediator between us,
someone who could bring us together.

³⁴ The mediator could make God stop beating me,
and I would no longer live in terror of his punishment.

³⁵ Then I could speak to him without fear,
but I cannot do that in my own strength.

10

JOB FRAMES HIS PLEA TO GOD

1 "I am disgusted with my life.
Let me complain freely.
My bitter soul must complain.

2 I will say to God, 'Don't simply condemn me—
tell me the charge you are bringing against me.

3 What do you gain by oppressing me?
Why do you reject me, the work of your own hands,
while smiling on the schemes of the wicked?

4 Are your eyes like those of a human?
Do you see things only as people see them?

5 Is your lifetime only as long as ours?
Is your life so short

6 that you must quickly probe for my guilt
and search for my sin?

7 Although you know I am not guilty,
no one can rescue me from your hands.

8 You formed me with your hands; you made me,
yet now you completely destroy me.

9 Remember that you made me from dust—
will you turn me back to dust so soon?

10 You guided my conception
and formed me in the womb.

11 You clothed me with skin and flesh,
and you knit my bones and sinews together.

12 You gave me life and showed me your unfailing love.
My life was preserved by your care.

13 Yet your real motive—
your true intent—

14 was to watch me, and if I sinned,
you would not forgive my guilt.

15 If I am guilty, too bad for me;
and even if I'm innocent, I can't hold my head high,
because I am filled with shame and misery.

16 And if I hold my head high, you hunt me like a lion
and display your awesome power against me.

17 Again and again you witness against me.
You pour out your growing anger on me
and bring fresh armies against me.

18 Why, then, did you deliver me from my mother's
womb? Why didn't you let me die at birth?

19 It would be as though I had never existed,

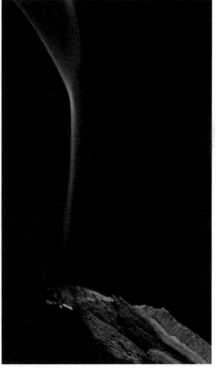

going directly from the womb to the grave.

[20] I have only a few days left, so leave me alone,
that I may have a moment of comfort

[21] before I leave—never to return—
for the land of darkness and utter gloom.

[22] It is a land as dark as midnight,
a land of gloom and confusion,
where even the light is dark as midnight.'"

11

ZOPHAR'S FIRST RESPONSE TO JOB

¹ Then Zophar the Naamathite replied to Job:

² "Shouldn't someone answer this torrent of words?
Is a person proved innocent just by a lot of talking?

³ Should I remain silent while you babble on?
When you mock God, shouldn't someone make
you ashamed?

⁴ You claim, 'My beliefs are pure,'
and 'I am clean in the sight of God.'

⁵ If only God would speak;
if only he would tell you what he thinks!

⁶ If only he would tell you the secrets of wisdom,
for true wisdom is not a simple matter.
Listen! God is doubtless punishing you
far less than you deserve!

⁷ Can you solve the mysteries of God?
Can you discover everything about the Almighty?

⁸ Such knowledge is higher than the heavens—
and who are you?
It is deeper than the underworld—
what do you know?

⁹ It is broader than the earth

and wider than the sea.

¹⁰ If God comes and puts a person in prison
or calls the court to order, who can stop him?

¹¹ For he knows those who are false,
and he takes note of all their sins.

¹² An empty-headed person won't become wise
any more than a wild donkey can bear a human child.

¹³ If only you would prepare your heart
and lift up your hands to him in prayer!

¹⁴ Get rid of your sins,
and leave all iniquity behind you.

¹⁵ Then your face will brighten with innocence.
You will be strong and free of fear.

¹⁶ You will forget your misery;
it will be like water flowing away.

¹⁷ Your life will be brighter than the noonday.
Even darkness will be as bright as morning.

¹⁸ Having hope will give you courage.
You will be protected and will rest in safety.

¹⁹ You will lie down unafraid,
and many will look to you for help.

²⁰ But the wicked will be blinded.
They will have no escape. Their only hope is death."

12

JOB'S FOURTH SPEECH: A RESPONSE TO ZOPHAR

¹ Then Job spoke again:

² "You people really know everything, don't you?
   And when you die, wisdom will die with you!
³ Well, I know a few things myself—
   and you're no better than I am.
   Who doesn't know these things you've been saying?
⁴ Yet my friends laugh at me,
   for I call on God and expect an answer.
   I am a just and blameless man,
   yet they laugh at me.
⁵ People who are at ease mock those in trouble.
   They give a push to people who are stumbling.
⁶ But robbers are left in peace,
   and those who provoke God live in safety—
   though God keeps them in his power.
⁷ Just ask the animals, and they will teach you.
   Ask the birds of the sky, and they will tell you.
⁸ Speak to the earth, and it will instruct you.
   Let the fish in the sea speak to you.

⁹ "For they all know
that my disaster has come from the hand of the Lord.

¹⁰ For the life of every living thing is in his hand,
and the breath of every human being.

¹¹ The ear tests the words it hears
just as the mouth distinguishes between foods.

¹² Wisdom belongs to the aged,
and understanding to the old.

¹³ But true wisdom and power are found in God;
counsel and understanding are his.

¹⁴ What he destroys cannot be rebuilt.
When he puts someone in prison, there is no escape.

¹⁵ If he holds back the rain, the earth becomes a desert.
If he releases the waters, they flood the earth.

¹⁶ Yes, strength and wisdom are his;
deceivers and deceived are both in his power.

¹⁷ He leads counselors away, stripped of good judgment;
wise judges become fools.

¹⁸ He removes the royal robe of kings.
They are led away with ropes around their waist.

¹⁹ He leads priests away, stripped of status;
he overthrows those with long years in power.

²⁰ He silences the trusted adviser
and removes the insight of the elders.

²¹ He pours disgrace upon princes
and disarms the strong.

²² He uncovers mysteries hidden in darkness;
he brings light to the deepest gloom.

²³ He builds up nations, and he destroys them.
He expands nations, and he abandons them.

²⁴ He strips kings of understanding
and leaves them wandering in a pathless wasteland.

²⁵ They grope in the darkness without a light.
He makes them stagger like drunkards.

13

JOB WANTS TO ARGUE HIS CASE WITH GOD

1 "Look, I have seen all this with my own eyes
and heard it with my own ears, and now I understand.

2 I know as much as you do.
You are no better than I am.

3 As for me, I would speak directly to the Almighty.
I want to argue my case with God himself.

4 As for you, you smear me with lies.
As physicians, you are worthless quacks.

5 If only you could be silent!
That's the wisest thing you could do.

6 Listen to my charge;
pay attention to my arguments.

7 Are you defending God with lies?
Do you make your dishonest arguments for his sake?

8 Will you slant your testimony in his favor?
Will you argue God's case for him?

9 What will happen when he finds out what you are
doing? Can you fool him as easily as you fool people?

10 No, you will be in trouble with him
if you secretly slant your testimony in his favor.

11 Doesn't his majesty terrify you?
Doesn't your fear of him overwhelm you?

12 Your platitudes are as valuable as ashes.
Your defense is as fragile as a clay pot.

13 Be silent now and leave me alone.
Let me speak, and I will face the consequences.

14 Why should I put myself in mortal danger
and take my life in my own hands?

15 God might kill me, but I have no other hope.
I am going to argue my case with him.

16 But this is what will save me—I am not godless.
If I were, I could not stand before him.

17 Listen closely to what I am about to say.
Hear me out.

18 I have prepared my case;
I will be proved innocent.

19 Who can argue with me over this?
And if you prove me wrong, I will remain
silent and die.

JOB ASKS HOW HE HAS SINNED

20 "O God, grant me these two things,

and then I will be able to face you.

21 Remove your heavy hand from me,

and don't terrify me with your awesome presence.

22 Now summon me, and I will answer!

Or let me speak to you, and you reply.

23 Tell me, what have I done wrong?

Show me my rebellion and my sin.

24 Why do you turn away from me?

Why do you treat me as your enemy?

25 Would you terrify a leaf blown by the wind?

Would you chase dry straw?

26 You write bitter accusations against me

and bring up all the sins of my youth.

27 You put my feet in stocks.

You examine all my paths.

You trace all my footprints.

28 I waste away like rotting wood,

like a moth-eaten coat.

CHAPTER 13

14

1 "How frail is humanity!
How short is life, how full of trouble!

2 We blossom like a flower and then wither.
Like a passing shadow, we quickly disappear.

3 Must you keep an eye on such a frail creature
and demand an accounting from me?

4 Who can bring purity out of an impure
person? No one!

5 You have decided the length of our lives.
You know how many months we will live,
and we are not given a minute longer.

6 So leave us alone and let us rest!
We are like hired hands, so let us finish our
work in peace.

7 Even a tree has more hope!
If it is cut down, it will sprout again
and grow new branches.

8 Though its roots have grown old in the earth
and its stump decays,

9 at the scent of water it will bud
and sprout again like a new seedling.

10 But when people die, their strength is gone.
They breathe their last, and then where are they?

11 As water evaporates from a lake
and a river disappears in drought,

12 people are laid to rest and do not rise again.
Until the heavens are no more, they will not wake up

nor be roused from their sleep.

13 I wish you would hide me in the grave
and forget me there until your anger has passed.
But mark your calendar to think of me again!

14 Can the dead live again?
If so, this would give me hope through all my
years of struggle,
and I would eagerly await the release of death.

15 You would call and I would answer,
and you would yearn for me, your handiwork.

16 For then you would guard my steps,
instead of watching for my sins.

17 My sins would be sealed in a pouch,
and you would cover my guilt.

18 But instead, as mountains fall and crumble
and as rocks fall from a cliff,

19 as water wears away the stones
and floods wash away the soil,
so you destroy people's hope.

20 You always overpower them, and they pass
from the scene.
You disfigure them in death and send them away.

21 They never know if their children grow up
in honor or
sink to insignificance.

22 They suffer painfully;
their life is full of trouble."

15

ELIPHAZ'S SECOND RESPONSE TO JOB

¹ Then Eliphaz the Temanite replied:

² "A wise man wouldn't answer with such empty talk!
You are nothing but a windbag.

³ The wise don't engage in empty chatter.
What good are such words?

⁴ Have you no fear of God,
no reverence for him?

⁵ Your sins are telling your mouth what to say.
Your words are based on clever deception.

⁶ Your own mouth condemns you, not I.
Your own lips testify against you.

⁷ Were you the first person ever born?
Were you born before the hills were made?

⁸ Were you listening at God's secret council?
Do you have a monopoly on wisdom?

⁹ What do you know that we don't?
What do you understand that we do not?

¹⁰ On our side are aged, gray-haired men
much older than your father!

11 Is God's comfort too little for you?
Is his gentle word not enough?

12 What has taken away your reason?
What has weakened your vision,

13 that you turn against God
and say all these evil things?

14 Can any mortal be pure?
Can anyone born of a woman be just?

15 Look, God does not even trust the angels.
Even the heavens are not absolutely pure in his sight.

16 How much less pure is a corrupt and sinful person
with a thirst for wickedness!

17 If you will listen, I will show you.
I will answer you from my own experience.

18 And it is confirmed by the reports of wise men
who have heard the same thing from their fathers—

19 from those to whom the land was given
long before any foreigners arrived.

20 The wicked writhe in pain throughout their lives.
Years of trouble are stored up for the ruthless.

21 The sound of terror rings in their ears,
and even on good days they fear the attack
of the destroyer.

22 They dare not go out into the darkness
for fear they will be murdered.

23 They wander around, saying, 'Where can
I find bread?'
They know their day of destruction is near.

24 That dark day terrifies them.
They live in distress and anguish,
like a king preparing for battle.

25 For they shake their fists at God,
defying the Almighty.

26 Holding their strong shields,
they defiantly charge against him.

27 These wicked people are heavy and prosperous;
their waists bulge with fat.

28 But their cities will be ruined.
They will live in abandoned houses
that are ready to tumble down.

29 Their riches will not last,
and their wealth will not endure.
Their possessions will no longer spread
across the horizon.

30 They will not escape the darkness.
The burning sun will wither their shoots,
and the breath of God will destroy them.

31 Let them no longer fool themselves by trusting in
empty riches,
for emptiness will be their only reward.

32 They will be cut down in the prime of life;
their branches will never again be green.

33 They will be like a vine whose grapes are
harvested too early,
like an olive tree that loses its blossoms before
the fruit can form.

34 For the godless are barren.
Their homes, enriched through bribery, will burn.

35 They conceive trouble and give birth to evil.
Their womb produces deceit."

16

JOB'S FIFTH SPEECH: A RESPONSE TO ELIPHAZ

1 Then Job spoke again:

2 "I have heard all this before.
What miserable comforters you are!

3 Won't you ever stop blowing hot air?
What makes you keep on talking?

4 I could say the same things if you were in my place.
I could spout off criticism and shake my head at you.

5 But if it were me, I would encourage you.
I would try to take away your grief.

6 Instead, I suffer if I defend myself,
and I suffer no less if I refuse to speak.

7 O God, you have ground me down
and devastated my family.

8 As if to prove I have sinned, you've reduced me to skin and bones.
My gaunt flesh testifies against me.

9 God hates me and angrily tears me apart.
He snaps his teeth at me
and pierces me with his eyes.

10 People jeer and laugh at me.
They slap my cheek in contempt.
A mob gathers against me.

11 God has handed me over to sinners.
He has tossed me into the hands of the wicked.

12 I was living quietly until he shattered me.
He took me by the neck and broke me in pieces.
Then he set me up as his target,

13 and now his archers surround me.
His arrows pierce me without mercy.
The ground is wet with my blood.

14 Again and again he smashes against me,
charging at me like a warrior.

15 I wear burlap to show my grief.
My pride lies in the dust.

16 My eyes are red with weeping;
dark shadows circle my eyes.

17 Yet I have done no wrong,
and my prayer is pure.

18 O earth, do not conceal my blood.
Let it cry out on my behalf.

19 Even now my witness is in heaven.
My advocate is there on high.

20 My friends scorn me,
but I pour out my tears to God.

21 I need someone to mediate between God and me,
as a person mediates between friends.

22 For soon I must go down that road
from which I will never return.

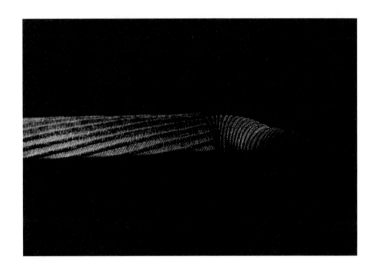

17

JOB CONTINUES TO DEFEND HIS INNOCENCE

1 "My spirit is crushed,
and my life is nearly snuffed out.
The grave is ready to receive me.

2 I am surrounded by mockers.
I watch how bitterly they taunt me.

3 You must defend my innocence, O God,
since no one else will stand up for me.

4 You have closed their minds to understanding,
but do not let them triumph.

5 They betray their friends for their own advantage,
so let their children faint with hunger.

6 God has made a mockery of me among the people;
they spit in my face.

7 My eyes are swollen with weeping,
and I am but a shadow of my former self.

8 The virtuous are horrified when they see me.
The innocent rise up against the ungodly.

9 The righteous keep moving forward,
and those with clean hands become stronger
and stronger.

10 As for all of you, come back with a better argument,
though I still won't find a wise man among you.

11 My days are over.
My hopes have disappeared.
My heart's desires are broken.

12 These men say that night is day;
they claim that the darkness is light.

13 What if I go to the grave
and make my bed in darkness?

14 What if I call the grave my father,
and the maggot my mother or my sister?

15 Where then is my hope?
Can anyone find it?

16 No, my hope will go down with me to the grave.
We will rest together in the dust!"

18

BILDAD'S SECOND RESPONSE TO JOB

¹ Then Bildad the Shuhite replied:

² "How long before you stop talking?
   Speak sense if you want us to answer!

³ Do you think we are mere animals?
   Do you think we are stupid?

⁴ You may tear out your hair in anger,
   but will that destroy the earth?
   Will it make the rocks tremble?

⁵ Surely the light of the wicked will be snuffed out.
   The sparks of their fire will not glow.

⁶ The light in their tent will grow dark.
   The lamp hanging above them will be quenched.

⁷ The confident stride of the wicked will be shortened.
   Their own schemes will be their downfall.

⁸ The wicked walk into a net.
   They fall into a pit.

⁹ A trap grabs them by the heel.
   A snare holds them tight.

¹⁰ A noose lies hidden on the ground.
    A rope is stretched across their path.

¹¹ Terrors surround the wicked
    and trouble them at every step.

¹² Hunger depletes their strength,
    and calamity waits for them to stumble.

¹³ Disease eats their skin;
    death devours their limbs.

¹⁴ They are torn from the security of their homes
    and are brought down to the king of terrors.

¹⁵ The homes of the wicked will burn down;
    burning sulfur rains on their houses.

¹⁶ Their roots will dry up,
    and their branches will wither.

¹⁷ All memory of their existence will fade from the earth;
    no one will remember their names.

¹⁸ They will be thrust from light into darkness,
    driven from the world.

¹⁹ They will have neither children nor grandchildren,
    nor any survivor in the place where they lived.

²⁰ People in the west are appalled at their fate;
    people in the east are horrified.

²¹ They will say, 'This was the home of a wicked person,
    the place of one who rejected God.'"

CHAPTER 18

19

JOB'S SIXTH SPEECH: A RESPONSE TO BILDAD

¹ Then Job spoke again:

² "How long will you torture me?
How long will you try to crush me with your words?

³ You have already insulted me ten times.
You should be ashamed of treating me so badly.

⁴ Even if I have sinned,
that is my concern, not yours.

⁵ You think you're better than I am,
using my humiliation as evidence of my sin.

⁶ But it is God who has wronged me,
capturing me in his net.

⁷ I cry out, 'Help!' but no one answers me.
I protest, but there is no justice.

⁸ God has blocked my way so I cannot move.
He has plunged my path into darkness.

⁹ He has stripped me of my honor
and removed the crown from my head.

¹⁰ He has demolished me on every side,
and I am finished.
He has uprooted my hope like a fallen tree.

¹¹ His fury burns against me;
he counts me as an enemy.

¹² His troops advance.
They build up roads to attack me.
They camp all around my tent.

¹³ My relatives stay far away,
and my friends have turned against me.

¹⁴ My family is gone,
and my close friends have forgotten me.

¹⁵ My servants and maids consider me a stranger.
I am like a foreigner to them.

¹⁶ When I call my servant, he doesn't come;
I have to plead with him!

¹⁷ My breath is repulsive to my wife.
I am rejected by my own family.

¹⁸ Even young children despise me.
When I stand to speak, they turn their backs on me.

¹⁹ My close friends detest me.
Those I loved have turned against me.

²⁰ I have been reduced to skin and bones
and have escaped death by the skin of my teeth.

²¹ Have mercy on me, my friends, have mercy,
for the hand of God has struck me.

²² Must you also persecute me, like God does?
Haven't you chewed me up enough?

²³ Oh, that my words could be recorded.
Oh, that they could be inscribed on a monument,

²⁴ carved with an iron chisel and filled with lead,
engraved forever in the rock.

²⁵ But as for me, I know that my Redeemer lives,
and he will stand upon the earth at last.

²⁶ And after my body has decayed,
yet in my body I will see God!

²⁷ I will see him for myself.
Yes, I will see him with my own eyes.
I am overwhelmed at the thought!

²⁸ How dare you go on persecuting me,
saying, 'It's his own fault'?

²⁹ You should fear punishment yourselves,
for your attitude deserves punishment.
Then you will know that there is
indeed a judgment."

20

ZOPHAR'S SECOND RESPONSE TO JOB

¹ Then Zophar the Naamathite replied:

² "I must reply
because I am greatly disturbed.
³ I've had to endure your insults,
but now my spirit prompts me to reply.
⁴ Don't you realize that from the beginning of time,
ever since people were first placed on the earth,
⁵ the triumph of the wicked has been short lived
and the joy of the godless has been only temporary?
⁶ Though the pride of the godless reaches to the heavens
and their heads touch the clouds,
⁷ yet they will vanish forever,
thrown away like their own dung.
Those who knew them will ask,
'Where are they?'
⁸ They will fade like a dream and not be found.
They will vanish like a vision in the night.
⁹ Those who once saw them will see them no more.
Their families will never see them again.
¹⁰ Their children will beg from the poor,
for they must give back their stolen riches.
¹¹ Though they are young,
their bones will lie in the dust.
¹² They enjoyed the sweet taste of wickedness,
letting it melt under their tongue.
¹³ They savored it,
holding it long in their mouths.
¹⁴ But suddenly the food in their bellies turns sour,
a poisonous venom in their stomach.
¹⁵ They will vomit the wealth they swallowed.
God won't let them keep it down.
¹⁶ They will suck the poison of cobras.
The viper will kill them.
¹⁷ They will never again enjoy streams of olive oil
or rivers of milk and honey.
¹⁸ They will give back everything they worked for.
Their wealth will bring them no joy.
¹⁹ For they oppressed the poor and left them destitute.
They foreclosed on their homes.
²⁰ They were always greedy and never satisfied.
Nothing remains of all the things they dreamed about.
²¹ Nothing is left after they finish gorging themselves.
Therefore, their prosperity will not endure.
²² In the midst of plenty, they will run into trouble
and be overcome by misery.
²³ May God give them a bellyful of trouble.
May God rain down his anger upon them.
²⁴ When they try to escape an iron weapon,
a bronze-tipped arrow will pierce them.
²⁵ The arrow is pulled from their back,
and the arrowhead glistens with blood.
The terrors of death are upon them.
²⁶ Their treasures will be thrown into
deepest darkness.
A wildfire will devour their goods,
consuming all they have left.
²⁷ The heavens will reveal their guilt,
and the earth will testify against them.
²⁸ A flood will sweep away their house.
God's anger will descend on them in torrents.
²⁹ This is the reward that God gives the wicked.
It is the inheritance decreed by God."

21

JOB'S SEVENTH SPEECH: A RESPONSE TO ZOPHAR

[1] Then Job spoke again:

[2] "Listen closely to what I am saying.
That's one consolation you can give me.

[3] Bear with me, and let me speak.
After I have spoken, you may resume mocking me.

[4] My complaint is with God, not with people.
I have good reason to be so impatient.

[5] Look at me and be stunned.
Put your hand over your mouth in shock.

[6] When I think about what I am saying, I shudder.
My body trembles.

⁷ Why do the wicked prosper,
   growing old and powerful?

⁸ They live to see their children grow up and settle
   down, and they enjoy their grandchildren.

⁹ Their homes are safe from every fear,
   and God does not punish them.

¹⁰ Their bulls never fail to breed.
   Their cows bear calves and never miscarry.

¹¹ They let their children frisk about like lambs.
   Their little ones skip and dance.

¹² They sing with tambourine and harp.
   They celebrate to the sound of the flute.

¹³ They spend their days in prosperity,
   then go down to the grave in peace.

¹⁴ And yet they say to God, 'Go away.
   We want no part of you and your ways.

¹⁵ Who is the Almighty, and why should we obey him?
   What good will it do us to pray?'

¹⁶ (They think their prosperity is of their own doing,
   but I will have nothing to do with that kind of thinking.)

¹⁷ Yet the light of the wicked never seems
   to be extinguished.
   Do they ever have trouble?
   Does God distribute sorrows to them in anger?

¹⁸ Are they driven before the wind like straw?
   Are they carried away by the storm like chaff?
   Not at all!

¹⁹ 'Well,' you say, 'at least God will punish
   their children!'
   But I say he should punish the ones who sin,
   so that they understand his judgment.

²⁰ Let them see their destruction with their own eyes.
Let them drink deeply of the anger of the Almighty.

²¹ For they will not care what happens to their family
after they are dead.

²² But who can teach a lesson to God,
since he judges even the most powerful?

²³ One person dies in prosperity,
completely comfortable and secure,

²⁴ the picture of good health,
vigorous and fit.

²⁵ Another person dies in bitter poverty,
never having tasted the good life.

²⁶ But both are buried in the same dust,
both eaten by the same maggots.

²⁷ Look, I know what you're thinking.
I know the schemes you plot against me.

²⁸ You will tell me of rich and wicked people
whose houses have vanished because of their sins.

²⁹ But ask those who have been around,
and they will tell you the truth.

³⁰ Evil people are spared in times of calamity
and are allowed to escape disaster.

³¹ No one criticizes them openly
or pays them back for what they have done.

³² When they are carried to the grave,
an honor guard keeps watch at their tomb.

³³ A great funeral procession goes to the cemetery.
Many pay their respects as the body is laid to rest,
and the earth gives sweet repose.

³⁴ How can your empty clichés comfort me?
All your explanations are lies!"

22

ELIPHAZ'S THIRD RESPONSE TO JOB

¹ Then Eliphaz the Temanite replied:

² "Can a person do anything to help God?
Can even a wise person be helpful to him?

³ Is it any advantage to the Almighty
if you are righteous?
Would it be any gain to him if you were perfect?

⁴ Is it because you're so pious that he accuses you
and brings judgment against you?

⁵ No, it's because of your wickedness!
There's no limit to your sins.

⁶ For example, you must have lent money to
your friend and demanded clothing as security.
Yes, you stripped him to the bone.

⁷ You must have refused water for the thirsty
and food for the hungry.

⁸ You probably think the land belongs to the powerful
and only the privileged have a right to it!

⁹ You must have sent widows away empty-handed
and crushed the hopes of orphans.

¹⁰ That is why you are surrounded by traps
and tremble from sudden fears.

¹¹ That is why you cannot see in the darkness,
and waves of water cover you.

¹² God is so great—higher than the heavens,
higher than the farthest stars.

¹³ But you reply, 'That's why God can't see what
I am doing!
How can he judge through the thick darkness?

¹⁴ For thick clouds swirl about him, and he
cannot see us.
He is way up there, walking on the vault of heaven.'

¹⁵ Will you continue on the old paths

where evil people have walked?

16 They were snatched away in the prime of life,
the foundations of their lives washed away.

17 For they said to God, 'Leave us alone!
What can the Almighty do to us?'

18 Yet he was the one who filled their homes with
good things,
so I will have nothing to do with that kind of thinking.

19 The righteous will be happy to see the
wicked destroyed,
and the innocent will laugh in contempt.

20 They will say, 'See how our enemies have
been destroyed.
The last of them have been consumed in the fire.'

21 Submit to God, and you will have peace;
then things will go well for you.

22 Listen to his instructions,

and store them in your heart.

23 If you return to the Almighty, you will be restored—
so clean up your life.

24 If you give up your lust for money
and throw your precious gold into the river,

25 the Almighty himself will be your treasure.
He will be your precious silver!

26 Then you will take delight in the Almighty
and look up to God.

27 You will pray to him, and he will hear you,
and you will fulfill your vows to him.

28 You will succeed in whatever you choose to do,
and light will shine on the road ahead of you.

29 If people are in trouble and you say, 'Help them,'
God will save them.

30 Even sinners will be rescued;
they will be rescued because your hands are pure."

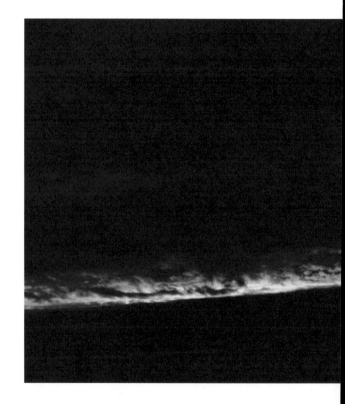

23

JOB'S EIGHTH SPEECH: A RESPONSE TO ELIPHAZ

¹ Then Job spoke again:

² "My complaint today is still a bitter one,
and I try hard not to groan aloud.
³ If only I knew where to find God,
I would go to his court.
⁴ I would lay out my case
and present my arguments.
⁵ Then I would listen to his reply
and understand what he says to me.
⁶ Would he use his great power to argue with me?
No, he would give me a fair hearing.
⁷ Honest people can reason with him,
so I would be forever acquitted by my judge.
⁸ I go east, but he is not there.
I go west, but I cannot find him.
⁹ I do not see him in the north, for he is hidden.
I look to the south, but he is concealed.
¹⁰ But he knows where I am going.
And when he tests me, I will come
out as pure as gold.
¹¹ For I have stayed on God's paths;
I have followed his ways and not turned aside.
¹² I have not departed from his commands,
but have treasured his words more than daily food.
¹³ But once he has made his decision, who can
change his mind?
Whatever he wants to do, he does.
¹⁴ So he will do to me whatever he has planned.
He controls my destiny.
¹⁵ No wonder I am so terrified in his presence.
When I think of it, terror grips me.
¹⁶ God has made me sick at heart;
the Almighty has terrified me.
¹⁷ Darkness is all around me;
thick, impenetrable
darkness is everywhere."

24

JOB ASKS WHY THE WICKED ARE NOT PUNISHED

1 "Why doesn't the Almighty bring the
wicked to judgment?
Why must the godly wait for him in vain?

2 Evil people steal land by moving the
boundary markers.
They steal livestock and put them
in their own pastures.

3 They take the orphan's donkey
and demand the widow's ox as security for a loan.

4 The poor are pushed off the path;
the needy must hide together for safety.

5 Like wild donkeys in the wilderness,
the poor must spend all their time looking for food,
searching even in the desert for food for their children.

6 They harvest a field they do not own,
and they glean in the vineyards of the wicked.

7 All night they lie naked in the cold,
without clothing or covering.

8 They are soaked by mountain showers,
and they huddle against the rocks
for want of a home.

9 The wicked snatch a widow's child from her breast,
taking the baby as security for a loan.

¹⁰ The poor must go about naked, without any clothing.
They harvest food for others while they
themselves are starving.

¹¹ They press out olive oil without being allowed to
taste it, and they tread in the winepress
as they suffer from thirst.

¹² The groans of the dying rise from the city,
and the wounded cry for help,
yet God ignores their moaning.

¹³ Wicked people rebel against the light.
They refuse to acknowledge its ways
or stay in its paths.

¹⁴ The murderer rises in the early dawn
to kill the poor and needy;
at night he is a thief.

¹⁵ The adulterer waits for the twilight,
saying, 'No one will see me then.'
He hides his face so no one will know him.

¹⁶ Thieves break into houses at night
and sleep in the daytime.
They are not acquainted with the light.

¹⁷ The black night is their morning.

They ally themselves with the terrors of the darkness.

¹⁸ But they disappear like foam down a river.
Everything they own is cursed,
and they are afraid to enter their own vineyards.

¹⁹ The grave consumes sinners
just as drought and heat consume snow.

²⁰ Their own mothers will forget them.
Maggots will find them sweet to eat.
No one will remember them.
Wicked people are broken like a tree in the storm.

²¹ They cheat the woman who has no son to help her.
They refuse to help the needy widow.

²² God, in his power, drags away the rich.
They may rise high, but they have
no assurance of life.

²³ They may be allowed to live in security,
but God is always watching them.

²⁴ And though they are great now,
in a moment they will be gone like all others,
cut off like heads of grain.

²⁵ Can anyone claim otherwise?
Who can prove me wrong?"

25

BILDAD'S THIRD RESPONSE TO JOB

[1] Then Bildad the Shuhite replied:

[2] "God is powerful and dreadful.
   He enforces peace in the heavens.
[3] Who is able to count his heavenly army?
   Doesn't his light shine on all the earth?
[4] How can a mortal be innocent before God?
   Can anyone born of a woman be pure?
[5] God is more glorious than the moon;
   he shines brighter than the stars.
[6] In comparison, people are maggots;
   we mortals are mere worms."

26

JOB'S NINTH SPEECH: A RESPONSE TO BILDAD

¹ Then Job spoke again:

² "How you have helped the powerless!
How you have saved the weak!
³ How you have enlightened my stupidity!
What wise advice you have offered!
⁴ Where have you gotten all these wise sayings?
Whose spirit speaks through you?
⁵ The dead tremble—
those who live beneath the waters.
⁶ The underworld is naked in God's presence.
The place of destruction is uncovered.
⁷ God stretches the northern sky over empty space
and hangs the earth on nothing.
⁸ He wraps the rain in his thick clouds,
and the clouds don't burst with the weight.
⁹ He covers the face of the moon,
shrouding it with his clouds.
¹⁰ He created the horizon when he separated the waters;
he set the boundary between day and night.
¹¹ The foundations of heaven tremble;
they shudder at his rebuke.
¹² By his power the sea grew calm.
By his skill he crushed the great sea monster.
¹³ His Spirit made the heavens beautiful,
and his power pierced the gliding serpent.
¹⁴ These are just the beginning of all that he does,
merely a whisper of his power.
Who, then, can comprehend the
thunder of his power?"

27

JOB'S FINAL SPEECH

¹ Job continued speaking:

² "I vow by the living God, who has taken away my
   rights, by the Almighty who has
   embittered my soul—
³ As long as I live,
   while I have breath from God,
⁴ my lips will speak no evil,
   and my tongue will speak no lies.
⁵ I will never concede that you are right;
   I will defend my integrity until I die.
⁶ I will maintain my innocence without wavering.
   My conscience is clear for as long as I live.
⁷ May my enemy be punished like the wicked,
   my adversary like those who do evil.
⁸ For what hope do the godless have when God cuts
   them off and takes away their life?
⁹ Will God listen to their cry
   when trouble comes upon them?
¹⁰ Can they take delight in the Almighty?
   Can they call to God at any time?
¹¹ I will teach you about God's power.
   I will not conceal anything concerning the Almighty.

¹² But you have seen all this,
yet you say all these useless things to me.

¹³ This is what the wicked will receive from God;
this is their inheritance from the Almighty.

¹⁴ They may have many children,
but the children will die in war or starve to death.

¹⁵ Those who survive will die of a plague,
and not even their widows will mourn them.

¹⁶ Evil people may have piles of money
and may store away mounds of clothing.

¹⁷ But the righteous will wear that clothing,
and the innocent will divide that money.

¹⁸ The wicked build houses as fragile as a spider's web,
as flimsy as a shelter made of branches.

¹⁹ The wicked go to bed rich
but wake to find that all their wealth is gone.

²⁰ Terror overwhelms them like a flood,
and they are blown away in the storms of the night.

²¹ The east wind carries them away, and they are gone.
It sweeps them away.

²² It whirls down on them without mercy.
They struggle to flee from its power.

²³ But everyone jeers at them
and mocks them.

28

JOB SPEAKS OF WISDOM AND UNDERSTANDING

1 "People know where to mine silver
and how to refine gold.

2 They know where to dig iron from the earth
and how to smelt copper from rock.

3 They know how to shine light in the darkness
and explore the farthest regions of the earth
as they search in the dark for ore.

4 They sink a mine shaft into the earth
far from where anyone lives.
They descend on ropes, swinging back and forth.

5 Food is grown on the earth above,
but down below, the earth is melted as by fire.

6 Here the rocks contain precious lapis lazuli,
and the dust contains gold.

7 These are treasures no bird of prey can see,
no falcon's eye observe.

8 No wild animal has walked upon these treasures;
no lion has ever set his paw there.

9 People know how to tear apart flinty rocks
and overturn the roots of mountains.

10 They cut tunnels in the rocks
and uncover precious stones.

11 They dam up the trickling streams
and bring to light the hidden treasures.

12 But do people know where to find wisdom?
Where can they find understanding?

13 No one knows where to find it,
for it is not found among the living.

14 'It is not here,' says the ocean.
'Nor is it here,' says the sea.

15 It cannot be bought with gold.

16 It cannot be purchased with silver.
It's worth more than all the gold of Ophir,
greater than precious onyx or lapis lazuli.

17 Wisdom is more valuable than gold and crystal.
It cannot be purchased with jewels
mounted in fine gold.

18 Coral and jasper are worthless in trying to get it.
The price of wisdom is far above rubies.

19 Precious peridot from Ethiopia cannot
be exchanged for it.
It's worth more than the purest gold.

20 But do people know where to find wisdom?
Where can they find understanding?

21 It is hidden from the eyes of all humanity.
Even the sharp-eyed birds in the sky
cannot discover it.

22 Destruction and Death say,
'We've heard only rumors of where
wisdom can be found.'

23 God alone understands the way to wisdom;
he knows where it can be found,

24 for he looks throughout the whole earth
and sees everything under the heavens.

25 He decided how hard the winds should blow
and how much rain should fall.

26 He made the laws for the rain
and laid out a path for the lightning.

27 Then he saw wisdom and evaluated it.
He set it in place and examined it thoroughly.

28 And this is what he says to all humanity:
'The fear of the Lord is true wisdom;
to forsake evil is real understanding.'"

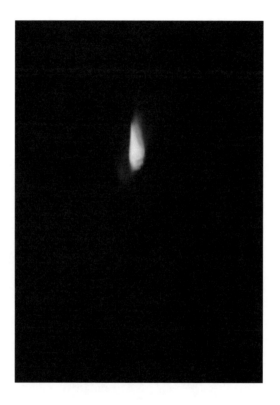

CHAPTER 28

29

JOB SPEAKS OF HIS FORMER BLESSINGS

¹ Job continued speaking:

² "I long for the years gone by
when God took care of me,
³ when he lit up the way before me
and I walked safely through the darkness.
⁴ When I was in my prime,
God's friendship was felt in my home.
⁵ The Almighty was still with me,
and my children were around me.
⁶ My steps were awash in cream,
and the rocks gushed olive oil for me.
⁷ Those were the days when I went to the city gate
and took my place among the honored leaders.
⁸ The young stepped aside when they saw me,
and even the aged rose in respect at my coming.
⁹ The princes stood in silence
and put their hands over their mouths.
¹⁰ The highest officials of the city stood quietly,
holding their tongues in respect.
¹¹ All who heard me praised me.
All who saw me spoke well of me.
¹² For I assisted the poor in their need
and the orphans who required help.
¹³ I helped those without hope, and they blessed me.
And I caused the widows' hearts to sing for joy.

¹⁴ Everything I did was honest.
Righteousness covered me like a robe,
and I wore justice like a turban.
¹⁵ I served as eyes for the blind
and feet for the lame.
¹⁶ I was a father to the poor
and assisted strangers who needed help.
¹⁷ I broke the jaws of godless oppressors
and plucked their victims from their teeth.
¹⁸ I thought, 'Surely I will die surrounded
by my family
after a long, good life.
¹⁹ For I am like a tree whose roots reach the water,
whose branches are refreshed with the dew.
²⁰ New honors are constantly bestowed on me,
and my strength is continually renewed.'
²¹ Everyone listened to my advice.
They were silent as they waited for me to speak.
²² And after I spoke, they had nothing to add,
for my counsel satisfied them.
²³ They longed for me to speak as people long for rain.
They drank my words like a refreshing spring rain.
²⁴ When they were discouraged, I smiled at them.
My look of approval was precious to them.
²⁵ Like a chief, I told them what to do.
I lived like a king among his troops
and comforted those who mourned."

30

JOB SPEAKS OF HIS ANGUISH

1 "But now I am mocked by people younger than I,
by young men whose fathers are not worthy to run
with my sheepdogs.

2 A lot of good they are to me—
those worn-out wretches!

3 They are gaunt from poverty and hunger.
They claw the dry ground in desolate wastelands.

4 They pluck wild greens from among the bushes
and eat from the roots of broom trees.

5 They are driven from human society,
and people shout at them as if they were thieves.

6 So now they live in frightening ravines,
in caves and among the rocks.

7 They sound like animals howling among the bushes,
huddled together beneath the nettles.

8 They are nameless fools,
outcasts from society.

9 And now they mock me with vulgar songs!
They taunt me!

10 They despise me and won't come near me,
except to spit in my face.

11 For God has cut my bowstring.
He has humbled me,
so they have thrown off all restraint.

12 These outcasts oppose me to my face.
They send me sprawling
and lay traps in my path.

¹³ They block my road

and do everything they can to destroy me.

They know I have no one to help me.

¹⁴ They come at me from all directions.

They jump on me when I am down.

¹⁵ I live in terror now.

My honor has blown away in the wind,

and my prosperity has vanished like a cloud.

¹⁶ And now my life seeps away.

Depression haunts my days.

¹⁷ At night my bones are filled with pain,

which gnaws at me relentlessly.

¹⁸ With a strong hand, God grabs my shirt.

He grips me by the collar of my coat.

¹⁹ He has thrown me into the mud.

I'm nothing more than dust and ashes.

²⁰ I cry to you, O God, but you don't answer.

I stand before you, but you don't even look.

²¹ You have become cruel toward me.

You use your power to persecute me.

²² You throw me into the whirlwind
and destroy me in the storm.

²³ And I know you are sending me to my death—
the destination of all who live.

²⁴ Surely no one would turn against the needy
when they cry for help in their trouble.

²⁵ Did I not weep for those in trouble?
Was I not deeply grieved for the needy?

²⁶ So I looked for good, but evil came instead.
I waited for the light, but darkness fell.

²⁷ My heart is troubled and restless.
Days of suffering torment me.

²⁸ I walk in gloom, without sunlight.
I stand in the public square and cry for help.

²⁹ Instead, I am considered a brother to jackals
and a companion to owls.

³⁰ My skin has turned dark,
and my bones burn with fever.

³¹ My harp plays sad music,
and my flute accompanies those who weep."

31

JOB'S FINAL PROTEST OF INNOCENCE

1 "I made a covenant with my eyes
not to look with lust at a young woman.

2 For what has God above chosen for us?
What is our inheritance from the Almighty on high?

3 Isn't it calamity for the wicked
and misfortune for those who do evil?

4 Doesn't he see everything I do
and every step I take?

5 Have I lied to anyone
or deceived anyone?

6 Let God weigh me on the scales of justice,
for he knows my integrity.

7 If I have strayed from his pathway,
or if my heart has lusted for what my eyes have seen,
or if I am guilty of any other sin,

8 then let someone else eat the crops I have planted.
Let all that I have planted be uprooted.

9 If my heart has been seduced by a woman,
or if I have lusted for my neighbor's wife,

10 then let my wife serve another man;
let other men sleep with her.

11 For lust is a shameful sin,
a crime that should be punished.

12 It is a fire that burns all the way to hell.
It would wipe out everything I own.

13 If I have been unfair to my male or female servants
when they brought their complaints to me,

14 how could I face God?
What could I say when he questioned me?

15 For God created both me and my servants.
He created us both in the womb.

16 Have I refused to help the poor,
or crushed the hopes of widows?

17 Have I been stingy with my food
and refused to share it with orphans?

18 No, from childhood I have cared for orphans
like a father,
and all my life I have cared for widows.

19 Whenever I saw the homeless without clothes
and the needy with nothing to wear,

20 did they not praise me
for providing wool clothing to keep them warm?

21 If I raised my hand against an orphan,
knowing the judges would take my side,

22 then let my shoulder be wrenched out of place!
Let my arm be torn from its socket!

23 That would be better than facing God's judgment.
For if the majesty of God opposes me,
what hope is there?

24 Have I put my trust in money
or felt secure because of my gold?

25 Have I gloated about my wealth
and all that I own?

26 Have I looked at the sun shining in the skies,
or the moon walking down its silver pathway,

27 and been secretly enticed in my heart
to throw kisses at them in worship?

28 If so, I should be punished by the judges,
for it would mean I had denied the God of heaven.

29 Have I ever rejoiced when disaster struck my enemies,
or become excited when harm came their way?

³⁰ No, I have never sinned by cursing anyone
    or by asking for revenge.
³¹ My servants have never said,
    'He let others go hungry.'
³² I have never turned away a stranger
    but have opened my doors to everyone.
³³ Have I tried to hide my sins like other people do,
    concealing my guilt in my heart?
³⁴ Have I feared the crowd
    or the contempt of the masses,
    so that I kept quiet and stayed indoors?
³⁵ If only someone would listen to me!
    Look, I will sign my name to my defense.
    Let the Almighty answer me.
    Let my accuser write out the charges against me.
³⁶ I would face the accusation proudly.
    I would wear it like a crown.
³⁷ For I would tell him exactly what I have done.
    I would come before him like a prince.
³⁸ If my land accuses me
    and all its furrows cry out together,
³⁹ or if I have stolen its crops
    or murdered its owners,
⁴⁰ then let thistles grow on that land instead of wheat,
    and weeds instead of barley."

Job's words are ended.

32

ELIHU RESPONDS TO JOB'S FRIENDS

¹ Job's three friends refused to reply further to him because he kept insisting on his innocence. ² Then Elihu son of Barakel the Buzite, of the clan of Ram, became angry. He was angry because Job refused to admit that he had sinned and that God was right in punishing him. ³ He was also angry with Job's three friends, for they made God appear to be wrong by their inability to answer Job's arguments. ⁴ Elihu had waited for the others to speak to Job because they were older than he. ⁵ But when he saw that they had no further reply, he spoke out angrily. ⁶ Elihu son of Barakel the Buzite said,

"I am young and you are old,
so I held back from telling you what I think.
⁷ I thought, 'Those who are older should speak,
for wisdom comes with age.'
⁸ But there is a spirit within people,
the breath of the Almighty within them,
that makes them intelligent.
⁹ Sometimes the elders are not wise.
Sometimes the aged do not understand justice.
¹⁰ So listen to me,
and let me tell you what I think.
¹¹ I have waited all this time,
listening very carefully to your arguments,
listening to you grope for words.
¹² I have listened,
but not one of you has refuted Job
or answered his arguments.
¹³ And don't tell me, 'He is too wise for us.
Only God can convince him.'
¹⁴ If Job had been arguing with me,
I would not answer with your kind of logic!
¹⁵ You sit there baffled,
with nothing more to say.
¹⁶ Should I continue to wait,
now that you are silent?
Must I also remain silent?
¹⁷ No, I will say my piece.
I will speak my mind.
¹⁸ For I am full of pent-up words,
and the spirit within me urges me on.
¹⁹ I am like a cask of wine without a vent,
like a new wineskin ready to burst!
²⁰ I must speak to find relief,
so let me give my answers.
²¹ I won't play favorites
or try to flatter anyone.
²² For if I tried flattery,
my Creator would soon destroy me."

33

ELIHU PRESENTS HIS CASE AGAINST JOB

1 "Listen to my words, Job;

pay attention to what I have to say.

2 Now that I have begun to speak,

let me continue.

3 I speak with all sincerity;

I speak the truth.

4 For the Spirit of God has made me,

and the breath of the Almighty gives me life.

5 Answer me, if you can;

make your case and take your stand.

6 Look, you and I both belong to God.

I, too, was formed from clay.

7 So you don't need to be afraid of me.

I won't come down hard on you.

8 You have spoken in my hearing,

and I have heard your very words.

9 You said, 'I am pure; I am without sin;

I am innocent; I have no guilt.

10 God is picking a quarrel with me,

and he considers me his enemy.

11 He puts my feet in the stocks

and watches my every move.'

12 But you are wrong, and I will show you why.

For God is greater than any human being.

¹³ So why are you bringing a charge against him?
   Why say he does not respond to people's complaints?
¹⁴ For God speaks again and again,
   though people do not recognize it.
¹⁵ He speaks in dreams, in visions of the night,
   when deep sleep falls on people
   as they lie in their beds.
¹⁶ He whispers in their ears
   and terrifies them with warnings.
¹⁷ He makes them turn from doing wrong;
   he keeps them from pride.
¹⁸ He protects them from the grave,

   from crossing over the river of death.
¹⁹ Or God disciplines people with pain on their sickbeds,
   with ceaseless aching in their bones.
²⁰ They lose their appetite
   for even the most delicious food.
²¹ Their flesh wastes away,
   and their bones stick out.
²² They are at death's door;
   the angels of death wait for them.
²³ But if an angel from heaven appears—
   a special messenger to intercede for a person
   and declare that he is upright—

CHAPTER 33

²⁴ he will be gracious and say,
  'Rescue him from the grave,
  for I have found a ransom for his life.'

²⁵ Then his body will become as healthy as a child's,
  firm and youthful again.

²⁶ When he prays to God,
  he will be accepted.
  And God will receive him with joy
  and restore him to good standing.

²⁷ He will declare to his friends,
  'I sinned and twisted the truth,
  but it was not worth it.

²⁸ God rescued me from the grave,
  and now my life is filled with light.'

²⁹ Yes, God does these things
  again and again for people.

³⁰ He rescues them from the grave
  so they may enjoy the light of life.

³¹ Mark this well, Job. Listen to me,
  for I have more to say.

³² But if you have anything to say, go ahead.
  Speak, for I am anxious to see you justified.

³³ But if not, then listen to me.
  Keep silent and I will teach you wisdom!"

34

ELIHU ACCUSES JOB OF ARROGANCE

¹ Then Elihu said:

² "Listen to me, you wise men.
Pay attention, you who have knowledge.

³ Job said, 'The ear tests the words it hears
just as the mouth distinguishes between foods.'

⁴ So let us discern for ourselves what is right;
let us learn together what is good.

⁵ For Job also said, 'I am innocent,
but God has taken away my rights.

⁶ I am innocent, but they call me a liar.
My suffering is incurable, though I have not sinned.'

⁷ Tell me, has there ever been a man like Job,
with his thirst for irreverent talk?

⁸ He chooses evil people as companions.
He spends his time with wicked men.

⁹ He has even said, 'Why waste time
trying to please God?'

¹⁰ Listen to me, you who have understanding.
Everyone knows that God doesn't sin!
The Almighty can do no wrong.

¹¹ He repays people according to their deeds.
He treats people as they deserve.

¹² Truly, God will not do wrong.
The Almighty will not twist justice.

¹³ Did someone else put the world in his care?
Who set the whole world in place?

¹⁴ If God were to take back his spirit
and withdraw his breath,

¹⁵ all life would cease,
and humanity would turn again to dust.

¹⁶ Now listen to me if you are wise.
Pay attention to what I say.

¹⁷ Could God govern if he hated justice?
Are you going to condemn the almighty judge?

¹⁸ For he says to kings, 'You are wicked,'
and to nobles, 'You are unjust.'

¹⁹ He doesn't care how great a person may be,
and he pays no more attention to the rich than
to the poor. He made them all.

²⁰ In a moment they die.
In the middle of the night they pass away;
the mighty are removed without human hand.

²¹ For God watches how people live;
he sees everything they do.

²² No darkness is thick enough
to hide the wicked from his eyes.

²³ We don't set the time
when we will come before God in judgment.

²⁴ He brings the mighty to ruin without asking anyone,
and he sets up others in their place.

²⁵ He knows what they do,
and in the night he overturns and destroys them.

²⁶ He strikes them down because they are wicked,
doing it openly for all to see.

²⁷ For they turned away from following him.
They have no respect for any of his ways.

²⁸ They cause the poor to cry out,
catching God's attention.
He hears the cries of the needy.

²⁹ But if he chooses to remain quiet,
who can criticize him?
When he hides his face, no one can find him,
whether an individual or a nation.

³⁰ He prevents the godless from ruling
so they cannot be a snare to the people.

³¹ Why don't people say to God, 'I have sinned,
but I will sin no more'?

³² Or 'I don't know what evil I have done—tell me.
If I have done wrong, I will stop at once'?

³³ Must God tailor his justice to your demands?
But you have rejected him!
The choice is yours, not mine.
Go ahead, share your wisdom with us.

³⁴ After all, bright people will tell me,
and wise people will hear me say,

³⁵ 'Job speaks out of ignorance;
his words lack insight.'

³⁶ Job, you deserve the maximum penalty
for the wicked way you have talked.

³⁷ For you have added rebellion to your sin;
you show no respect,
and you speak many angry words against God."

35

ELIHU REMINDS JOB OF GOD'S JUSTICE

¹ Then Elihu said:

² "Do you think it is right for you to claim,
'I am righteous before God'?

³ For you also ask, 'What's in it for me?
What's the use of living a righteous life?'

⁴ I will answer you
and all your friends, too.

⁵ Look up into the sky,
and see the clouds high above you.

⁶ If you sin, how does that affect God?
Even if you sin again and again,
what effect will it have on him?

⁷ If you are good, is this some great gift to him?
What could you possibly give him?

⁸ No, your sins affect only people like yourself,
and your good deeds also affect only humans.

⁹ People cry out when they are oppressed.
They groan beneath the power of the mighty.

¹⁰ Yet they don't ask,
'Where is God my Creator,
the one who gives songs in the night?

¹¹ Where is the one who makes us smarter
than the animals
and wiser than the birds of the sky?'

¹² And when they cry out, God does not answer
because of their pride.

¹³ But it is wrong to say God doesn't listen,
to say the Almighty isn't concerned.

¹⁴ You say you can't see him,
but he will bring justice if you will only wait.

¹⁵ You say he does not respond to sinners with anger
and is not greatly concerned about wickedness.

¹⁶ But you are talking nonsense, Job.
You have spoken like a fool."

CHAPTER 35

36

¹ Elihu continued speaking:

² "Let me go on, and I will show you the truth.
For I have not finished defending God!

³ I will present profound arguments
for the righteousness of my Creator.

⁴ I am telling you nothing but the truth,
for I am a man of great knowledge.

⁵ God is mighty, but he does not despise anyone!
He is mighty in both power and understanding.

⁶ He does not let the wicked live
but gives justice to the afflicted.

⁷ He never takes his eyes off the innocent,
but he sets them on thrones with kings
and exalts them forever.

⁸ If they are bound in chains
and caught up in a web of trouble,

⁹ he shows them the reason.
He shows them their sins of pride.

¹⁰ He gets their attention
and commands that they turn from evil.

¹¹ If they listen and obey God,
they will be blessed with prosperity
throughout their lives.
All their years will be pleasant.

¹² But if they refuse to listen to him,

they will cross over the river of death,
dying from lack of understanding.

¹³ For the godless are full of resentment.
Even when he punishes them,
they refuse to cry out to him for help.

¹⁴ They die when they are young,
after wasting their lives in immoral living.

¹⁵ But by means of their suffering, he rescues
those who suffer.
For he gets their attention through adversity.

¹⁶ God is leading you away from danger, Job,
to a place free from distress.
He is setting your table with the best food.

¹⁷ But you are obsessed with whether the
godless will be judged.
Don't worry, judgment and justice will be upheld.

¹⁸ But watch out, or you may be seduced by wealth.
Don't let yourself be bribed into sin.

¹⁹ Could all your wealth
or all your mighty efforts
keep you from distress?

²⁰ Do not long for the cover of night,
for that is when people will be destroyed.

²¹ Be on guard! Turn back from evil,
for God sent this suffering
to keep you from a life of evil.

ELIHU REMINDS JOB OF GOD'S POWER

22 "Look, God is all-powerful.
Who is a teacher like him?

23 No one can tell him what to do,
or say to him, 'You have done wrong.'

24 Instead, glorify his mighty works,
singing songs of praise.

25 Everyone has seen these things,
though only from a distance.

26 Look, God is greater than we can understand.
His years cannot be counted.

27 He draws up the water vapor
and then distills it into rain.

28 The rain pours down from the clouds,
and everyone benefits.

29 Who can understand the spreading of the clouds
and the thunder that rolls forth from heaven?

30 See how he spreads the lightning around him
and how it lights up the depths of the sea.

31 By these mighty acts he nourishes the people,
giving them food in abundance.

32 He fills his hands with lightning bolts
and hurls each at its target.

33 The thunder announces his presence;
the storm announces his indignant anger.

37

¹ "My heart pounds as I think of this.
It trembles within me.
² Listen carefully to the thunder of God's voice
as it rolls from his mouth.
³ It rolls across the heavens,
and his lightning flashes in every direction.
⁴ Then comes the roaring of the thunder—
the tremendous voice of his majesty.
He does not restrain it when he speaks.

⁵ God's voice is glorious in the thunder.
We can't even imagine the greatness of his power.
⁶ He directs the snow to fall on the earth
and tells the rain to pour down.
⁷ Then everyone stops working
so they can watch his power.
⁸ The wild animals take cover
and stay inside their dens.
⁹ The stormy wind comes from its chamber,

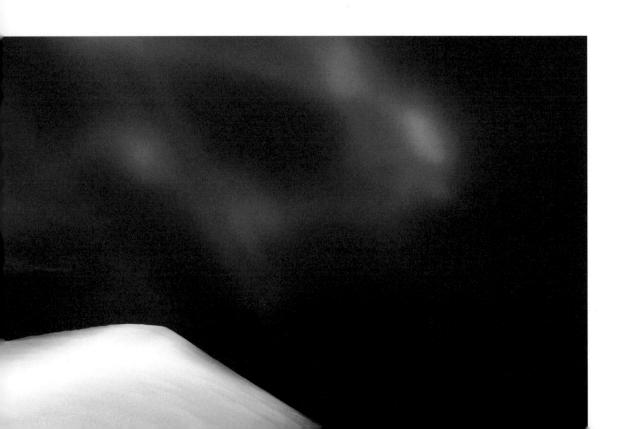

and the driving winds bring the cold.

¹⁰ God's breath sends the ice,
freezing wide expanses of water.

¹¹ He loads the clouds with moisture,
and they flash with his lightning.

¹² The clouds churn about at his direction.
They do whatever he commands
throughout the earth.

¹³ He makes these things happen either to punish people

or to show his unfailing love.

¹⁴ Pay attention to this, Job.
Stop and consider the wonderful miracles of God!

¹⁵ Do you know how God controls the storm
and causes the lightning to flash from his clouds?

¹⁶ Do you understand how he moves the clouds
with wonderful perfection and skill?

¹⁷ When you are sweltering in your clothes
and the south wind dies down and everything is still,

CHAPTER 37

18   he makes the skies reflect the heat like
     a bronze mirror. Can you do that?
19   So teach the rest of us what to say to God.
     We are too ignorant to make our own arguments.
20   Should God be notified that I want to speak?
     Can people even speak when they are confused?
21   We cannot look at the sun,
     for it shines brightly in the sky
     when the wind clears away the clouds.
22   So also, golden splendor comes from the
     mountain of God.
     He is clothed in dazzling splendor.
23   We cannot imagine the power of the Almighty;
     but even though he is just and righteous,
     he does not destroy us.
24   No wonder people everywhere fear him.
     All who are wise show him reverence."

38

THE LORD CHALLENGES JOB

¹ Then the Lord answered Job from the whirlwind:

² "Who is this that questions my wisdom
with such ignorant words?

³ Brace yourself like a man,
because I have some questions for you,
and you must answer them.

⁴ Where were you when I laid the foundations
of the earth?
Tell me, if you know so much.

⁵ Who determined its dimensions
and stretched out the surveying line?

⁶ What supports its foundations,
and who laid its cornerstone

⁷ as the morning stars sang together
and all the angels shouted for joy?

⁸ Who kept the sea inside its boundaries
as it burst from the womb,

⁹ and as I clothed it with clouds
and wrapped it in thick darkness?

¹⁰ For I locked it behind barred gates,
limiting its shores.

¹¹ I said, 'This far and no farther will you come.
Here your proud waves must stop!'

¹² Have you ever commanded the morning to appear
and caused the dawn to rise in the east?

¹³ Have you made daylight spread to the ends
of the earth,
to bring an end to the night's wickedness?

¹⁴ As the light approaches,
the earth takes shape like clay pressed beneath a seal;
it is robed in brilliant colors.

¹⁵ The light disturbs the wicked
and stops the arm that is raised in violence.

¹⁶ Have you explored the springs from
which the seas come?
Have you explored their depths?

¹⁷ Do you know where the gates of death are located?
Have you seen the gates of utter gloom?

¹⁸ Do you realize the extent of the earth?
Tell me about it if you know!

¹⁹ Where does light come from,
and where does darkness go?

²⁰ Can you take each to its home?
Do you know how to get there?

²¹ But of course you know all this!
   For you were born before it was all created,
   and you are so very experienced!
²² Have you visited the storehouses of the snow
   or seen the storehouses of hail?
²³ (I have reserved them as weapons for the
   time of trouble,
   for the day of battle and war.)
²⁴ Where is the path to the source of light?
   Where is the home of the east wind?
²⁵ Who created a channel for the torrents of rain?
   Who laid out the path for the lightning?
²⁶ Who makes the rain fall on barren land,
   in a desert where no one lives?
²⁷ Who sends rain to satisfy the parched ground
   and make the tender grass spring up?
²⁸ Does the rain have a father?
   Who gives birth to the dew?
²⁹ Who is the mother of the ice?
   Who gives birth to the frost from the heavens?
³⁰ For the water turns to ice as hard as rock,
   and the surface of the water freezes.
³¹ Can you direct the movement of the stars—

binding the cluster of the Pleiades
   or loosening the cords of Orion?
³² Can you direct the constellations through the seasons
   or guide the Bear with her cubs across the heavens?
³³ Do you know the laws of the universe?
   Can you use them to regulate the earth?
³⁴ Can you shout to the clouds
   and make it rain?
³⁵ Can you make lightning appear
   and cause it to strike as you direct?
³⁶ Who gives intuition to the heart
   and instinct to the mind?
³⁷ Who is wise enough to count all the clouds?
   Who can tilt the water jars of heaven
³⁸ when the parched ground is dry
   and the soil has hardened into clods?
³⁹ Can you stalk prey for a lioness
   and satisfy the young lions' appetites
⁴⁰ as they lie in their dens
   or crouch in the thicket?
⁴¹ Who provides food for the ravens
   when their young cry out to God
   and wander about in hunger?"

39

THE LORD'S CHALLENGE CONTINUES

1 "Do you know when the wild goats give birth?
Have you watched as deer are born in the wild?

2 Do you know how many months they
carry their young?
Are you aware of the time of their delivery?

3 They crouch down to give birth to their young
and deliver their offspring.

4 Their young grow up in the open fields,
then leave home and never return.

5 Who gives the wild donkey its freedom?
Who untied its ropes?

6 I have placed it in the wilderness;
its home is the wasteland.

7 It hates the noise of the city
and has no driver to shout at it.

8 The mountains are its pastureland,

where it searches for every blade of grass.

9 Will the wild ox consent to being tamed?
Will it spend the night in your stall?

10 Can you hitch a wild ox to a plow?
Will it plow a field for you?

11 Given its strength, can you trust it?
Can you leave and trust the ox to do your work?

12 Can you rely on it to bring home your grain
and deliver it to your threshing floor?

13 The ostrich flaps her wings grandly,
but they are no match for
the feathers of the stork.

14 She lays her eggs on top of the earth,
letting them be warmed in the dust.

15 She doesn't worry that a foot might crush them
or a wild animal might destroy them.

16 She is harsh toward her young,

as if they were not her own.
She doesn't care if they die.

17 For God has deprived her of wisdom.
He has given her no understanding.

18 But whenever she jumps up to run,
she passes the swiftest horse with its rider.

19 Have you given the horse its strength
or clothed its neck with a flowing mane?

20 Did you give it the ability to leap like a locust?
Its majestic snorting is terrifying!

21 It paws the earth and rejoices in its strength
when it charges out to battle.

22 It laughs at fear and is unafraid.
It does not run from the sword.

23 The arrows rattle against it,
and the spear and javelin flash.

24 It paws the ground fiercely

and rushes forward into battle when the
ram's horn blows.

25 It snorts at the sound of the horn.
It senses the battle in the distance.
It quivers at the captain's commands and
the noise of battle.

26 Is it your wisdom that makes the hawk soar
and spread its wings toward the south?

27 Is it at your command that the eagle rises
to the heights to make its nest?

28 It lives on the cliffs,
making its home on a distant, rocky crag.

29 From there it hunts its prey,
keeping watch with piercing eyes.

30 Its young gulp down blood.
Where there's a carcass,
there you'll find it."

40

¹ Then the Lord said to Job,

² "Do you still want to argue with the Almighty?
You are God's critic, but do you have the answers?"

JOB RESPONDS TO THE LORD

³ Then Job replied to the Lord,

⁴ "I am nothing—how could I ever find the answers?
I will cover my mouth with my hand.
⁵ I have said too much already.
I have nothing more to say."

THE LORD CHALLENGES JOB AGAIN

⁶ Then the Lord answered Job from the whirlwind:

⁷ "Brace yourself like a man,
because I have some questions for you,
and you must answer them.
⁸ Will you discredit my justice
and condemn me just to prove you are right?
⁹ Are you as strong as God?
Can you thunder with a voice like his?
¹⁰ All right, put on your glory and splendor,
your honor and majesty.
¹¹ Give vent to your anger.
Let it overflow against the proud.
¹² Humiliate the proud with a glance;

walk on the wicked where they stand.
¹³ Bury them in the dust.
Imprison them in the world of the dead.
¹⁴ Then even I would praise you,
for your own strength would save you.
¹⁵ Take a look at Behemoth,
which I made, just as I made you.
It eats grass like an ox.
¹⁶ See its powerful loins
and the muscles of its belly.
¹⁷ Its tail is as strong as a cedar.
The sinews of its thighs are knit tightly together.
¹⁸ Its bones are tubes of bronze.
Its limbs are bars of iron.
¹⁹ It is a prime example of God's handiwork,
and only its Creator can threaten it.
²⁰ The mountains offer it their best food,
where all the wild animals play.
²¹ It lies under the lotus plants,
hidden by the reeds in the marsh.
²² The lotus plants give it shade
among the willows beside the stream.
²³ It is not disturbed by the raging river,
not concerned when the swelling Jordan
rushes around it.
²⁴ No one can catch it off guard
or put a ring in its nose
and lead it away."

41

THE LORD'S CHALLENGE CONTINUES

1 "Can you catch Leviathan with a hook
or put a noose around its jaw?

2 Can you tie it with a rope through the nose
or pierce its jaw with a spike?

3 Will it beg you for mercy
or implore you for pity?

4 Will it agree to work for you,
to be your slave for life?

5 Can you make it a pet like a bird,
or give it to your little girls to play with?

6 Will merchants try to buy it
to sell it in their shops?

7 Will its hide be hurt by spears
or its head by a harpoon?

8 If you lay a hand on it,
you will certainly remember the battle that follows.
You won't try that again!

9 No, it is useless to try to capture it.
The hunter who attempts it will be knocked down.

10 And since no one dares to disturb it,
who then can stand up to me?

11 Who has given me anything that I need to pay back?
Everything under heaven is mine.

12 I want to emphasize Leviathan's limbs
and its enormous strength and graceful form.

13 Who can strip off its hide,
and who can penetrate its double layer of armor?

14 Who could pry open its jaws?
For its teeth are terrible!

15 The scales on its back are like rows of shields
tightly sealed together.

16 They are so close together
that no air can get between them.

17 Each scale sticks tight to the next.
They interlock and cannot be penetrated.

18 When it sneezes, it flashes light!
Its eyes are like the red of dawn.

19 Lightning leaps from its mouth;
flames of fire flash out.

20 Smoke streams from its nostrils
like steam from a pot heated over burning rushes.

CHAPTER 41

²¹ Its breath would kindle coals,
for flames shoot from its mouth.

²² The tremendous strength in Leviathan's neck
strikes terror wherever it goes.

²³ Its flesh is hard and firm
and cannot be penetrated.

²⁴ Its heart is hard as rock,
hard as a millstone.

²⁵ When it rises, the mighty are afraid,
gripped by terror.

²⁶ No sword can stop it,
no spear, dart, or javelin.

²⁷ Iron is nothing but straw to that creature,
and bronze is like rotten wood.

²⁸ Arrows cannot make it flee.
Stones shot from a sling are like bits of grass.

²⁹ Clubs are like a blade of grass,
and it laughs at the swish of javelins.

³⁰ Its belly is covered with scales as sharp as glass.
It plows up the ground as it drags through the mud.

³¹ Leviathan makes the water boil with its commotion.
It stirs the depths like a pot of ointment.

³² The water glistens in its wake,
making the sea look white.

³³ Nothing on earth is its equal,
no other creature so fearless.

³⁴ Of all the creatures, it is the proudest.
It is the king of beasts."

42

JOB RESPONDS TO THE LORD

¹ Then Job replied to the Lord:

² "I know that you can do anything,
    and no one can stop you.
³ You asked, 'Who is this that questions my wisdom
    with such ignorance?'
    It is I—and I was talking about things I
    knew nothing about,
    things far too wonderful for me.
⁴ You said, 'Listen and I will speak!
    I have some questions for you,
    and you must answer them.'
⁵ I had only heard about you before,
    but now I have seen you with my own eyes.
⁶ I take back everything I said,
    and I sit in dust and ashes to show my repentance."

CONCLUSION: THE LORD BLESSES JOB

[7] After the Lord had finished speaking to Job, he said to Eliphaz the Temanite: "I am angry with you and your two friends, for you have not spoken accurately about me, as my servant Job has. [8] So take seven bulls and seven rams and go to my servant Job and offer a burnt offering for yourselves. My servant Job will pray for you, and I will accept his prayer on your behalf. I will not treat you as you deserve, for you have not spoken accurately about me, as my servant Job has." [9] So Eliphaz the Temanite, Bildad the Shuhite, and Zophar the Naamathite did as the Lord commanded them, and the Lord accepted Job's prayer. [10] When Job prayed for his friends, the Lord restored his fortunes. In fact, the Lord gave him twice as much as before! [11] Then all his brothers, sisters, and former friends came and feasted with him in his home. And they consoled him and comforted him because of all the trials the Lord had brought against him. And each of them brought him a gift of money and a gold ring. [12] So the Lord blessed Job in the second half of his life even more than in the beginning. For now he had 14,000 sheep, 6,000 camels, 1,000 teams of oxen, and 1,000 female donkeys. [13] He also gave Job seven more sons and three more daughters. [14] He named his first daughter Jemimah, the second Keziah, and the third Keren-happuch. [15] In all the land no women were as lovely as the daughters of Job. And their father put them into his will along with their brothers. [16] Job lived 140 years after that, living to see four generations of his children and grandchildren. [17] Then he died, an old man who had lived a long, full life.

ALABASTER

TYLER ZAK
Product Manager, Art Director

MATTHEW RAVENELLE
Layout Designer

SAMUEL HAN
Studio Photographer, Photography Editor

MARK YEONGJUN SEO
Studio Stylist

ALEXIS SOOMIN LEE
Studio Assistant

JONATHAN KNEPPER
Cover Image

BRYAN YE-CHUNG
Co-Founder, Creative Director

BRIAN CHUNG
Co-Founder, Managing Director

WILLA JIN
Operations Director

EMALY HUNTER
Customer Experience Specialist

DARIN MCKENNA
Content Editor

JOSEPHINE LAW
Original Designer

ALABASTER

PHOTOGRAPHERS

Andriana Kovalchuk
Bryan Ye-Chung
Heidi Parra
Isaiah Im
Jacob Chung
Joel Rojas
Jonathan Knepper
Joshua Martens
Lois Lee

Makito Umekita
Marissa Honjiyo
Mike Sunu
Peter Kang
Samuel Han
Stephen Rheeder
Tirza Hartono
Tyler Zak

MODELS

Alexis Soomin Lee
Mark Yeongjun Seo

PAINTINGS

Bryan Ye-Chung

CONTINUE THE CONVERSATION
www.alabasterco.com